THE STORY OF THE
SEATTLE SEAHAWKS

NFL TODAY

THE STORY OF THE SEATTLE SEAHAWKS

SARA GILBERT

CREATIVE EDUCATION

Cover: Linebacker Julian Peterson (top), running back Julius Jones (bottom)
Page 2: Running back T. J. Duckett
Pages 4–5: Qwest Field
Pages 6–7: 2007 Seattle Seahawks

....

Published by Creative Education
P.O. Box 227, Mankato, Minnesota 56002
Creative Education is an imprint of
The Creative Company
www.thecreativecompany.us

Design and production by Blue Design
Design Associate: Sarah Yakawonis
Printed in the United States of America

Photographs by Corbis (Bettmann, Jose Fuste
Raga, Troy Wayrynen/Columbian/NewSport), Getty
Images (Al Bello, Jonathan Daniel, Miqual A. Ellliot/
NFL, George Gojkovich, Steve Grayson/NFL, Otto
Greule Jr, Otto Greule Jr./Allsport, Tom Hauck, Jed
Jacobsohn, Jed Jacobsohn/Allsport, Paul Jasienski,
Craig Jones, NFL, NFL Photos, Mike Powell, Rick
Stewart, Kevin Terrell, Kevin Terrell/NFL Photos,
Corky Charles Trewin/NFL, Greg Trott, Greg Trott/
NFL, Maxx Wolfson)

Library of Congress Cataloging-in-Publication Data

Gilbert, Sara.
The story of the Seattle Seahawks / Sara Gilbert.
p. cm. — (NFL today)
Includes index.
ISBN 978-1-58341-771-3
1. Seattle Seahawks (Football team)—History—
Juvenile literature. I. Title. II. Series.

GV956.S4G56 2009
796.332'6409797772—dc22   2008022703

First Edition
9 8 7 6 5 4 3 2 1

CONTENTS

ON THE SIDELINES

MEET THE SEAHAWKS

A SOARING START

X

When American settlers first reached Seattle, Washington, in the 1850s, they found a forest of 400-foot-tall trees, many of which had been standing there for more than 1,000 years. Those towering trees gave birth to the booming logging industry that sustained the city in its early days. Many of those trees have since been cut down, and their replacements have not grown as tall. Seattle is now better known for its aerospace and technology businesses, but it has always maintained a connection to the natural resources so plentiful in the region surrounding the city.

I t was no surprise, then, that when the National Football League (NFL) granted Seattle an expansion franchise in 1974, the public overwhelmingly voted to name the new team the Seahawks after the large, powerful birds that are native to the coastal areas of the Pacific Northwest. And for the three decades that the team has been in Seattle, fans have flocked to see those Seahawks play in the shadows of those once-towering trees.

The first Seahawks team was made up primarily of veteran castoffs who were nearing the ends of their careers—such as Bob Lurtsema, a defensive end plucked from the Minnesota Vikings—and young, unproven talents chosen from the NFL Draft. But when head coach Jack Patera looked over his roster

X Seattle's famed Space Needle is a remnant from the 1962 World's Fair, a six-month-long event that introduced the city to the world a decade before the Seahawks franchise was born.

in 1976, he made a bold prediction for the new Seattle team: it would achieve a 12–2 record.

Things didn't work out the way Patera had planned. After opening the season 0–5, the Seahawks met the Tampa Bay Buccaneers—another expansion team with an identical record—in Week 6 of the 1976 season. It was an ugly game that included 35 total penalties. The saving grace, however, was that it didn't go into overtime. When the Buccaneers sent their kicking unit in to try for a game-tying field goal with 42 seconds left on the clock, burly Seahawks linebacker Mike Curtis blocked the kick. That 13–10 victory was Seattle's first and one of only two wins the team would enjoy in its inaugural season.

Although wins were few, optimism ran high. Fans immediately sensed the chemistry building among the young Seahawks players, especially between quarterback Jim Zorn and his favorite downfield target, wide receiver Steve Largent. Zorn threw for almost 2,600 yards and earned Offensive Rookie of the Year honors in 1976, and Largent showed signs of future stardom by posting 705 receiving yards and 4 touchdowns. Running back Sherman Smith, who rushed for 124 yards in a late-season game, also gave Seattle fans reason to believe in a bright future.

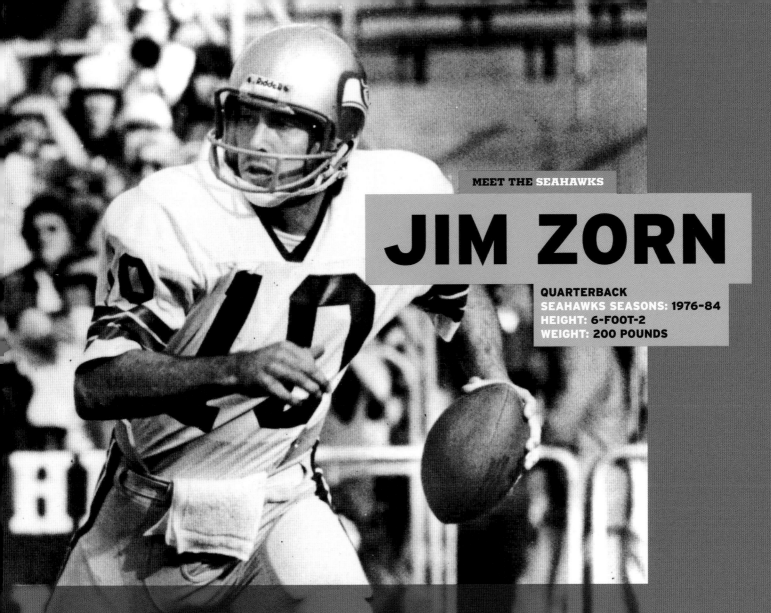

JIM ZORN

QUARTERBACK
SEAHAWKS SEASONS: 1976-84
HEIGHT: 6-FOOT-2
WEIGHT: 200 POUNDS

Jim Zorn was the perfect fit as the first quarterback for the Seattle Seahawks' first season. Like the new team, Zorn was young, energetic, and eager to improve. And although he immediately made his mark as a rookie, when he earned team Most Valuable Player (MVP) and conference Offensive Rookie of the Year honors, he and the Seahawks collectively improved during his tenure with the team. By 1979, he had almost doubled his touchdown production and increased his passing totals by about 1,000 yards. His arm was amazingly accurate, and his feet were frighteningly quick; when he wasn't passing the football, he was frequently running with it. Most often, however, Zorn was directing the ball into the hands of receiver Steve Largent, the young quarterback's favorite downfield target. By the time Zorn left Seattle, he had amassed a total of 20,122 passing yards and 107 touchdown passes. "I'm just happy to be a Seahawk as long as I was," Zorn said. "I wish it would have been longer." In 2008, he was hired as head coach of the Washington Redskins.

SEATTLE HAS A SAY

Although a group of local business leaders became the official owners of the new NFL franchise in Seattle in 1974, the owners made it clear that the team would belong to the city as well. The team's name, they said, would be chosen by popular vote. And the popular choice turned out to be Seahawks, one of more than 1,700 different names submitted by more than 20,000 people. But while putting the team's name to a vote has been fairly typical of NFL franchises, letting fans decide what color the team's helmets should be is not. In 2002, when the Seahawks moved to their new home at Qwest Field, the team unveiled new uniforms as well. The plan was to wear silver helmets for home games and blue helmets on the road—but NFL rules prohibit the use of alternate-colored helmets by one team. So once again, the Seahawks turned to the fans with a question: Which helmets should they wear? The fans selected "Seahawks Blue," a color that can appear gray, navy, or even turquoise, depending on the lighting.

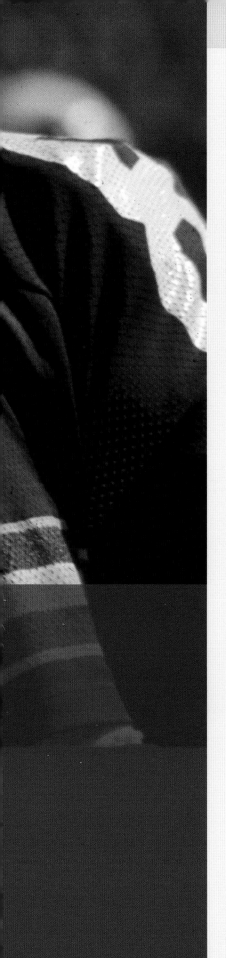

As those young players gained experience, the Seahawks quickly climbed the standings in the American Football Conference (AFC) West Division. Seattle jumped to 5–9 in 1977, then posted back-to-back 9–7 records in 1978 and 1979. Patera's creative play-calling made national news after Seattle's first Monday Night Football appearance in October 1979. The Seahawks came back from a 14–0 deficit to beat the Atlanta Falcons 31–28, thanks in part to a fake field goal pass from Zorn to kicker Efren Herrera. As legendary broadcaster Howard Cosell watched the play unfold, he proclaimed, "The Seahawks are giving the nation a lesson in entertaining football!"

With Zorn launching long passes to both Largent and scrappy wide receiver Sam McCullum, and Smith anchoring the running game, the Seahawks did make it look fun. Largent was easily collecting 1,000 or more receiving yards a season and had been selected to play in the Pro Bowl for 2 consecutive years. But things got tougher in 1980. After defeating the New York Jets 27–17 in mid-October, the Seahawks went winless for the rest of the season. Zorn threw 20 interceptions as the team dropped to 4–12, falling into last place in the AFC West.

Despite the additions of safety Kenny Easley and running back Theotis Brown, the 1981 Seahawks struggled from the

Both big and speedy, Kenny Easley (number 45) was one of Seattle's first true stars, earning All-Pro honors (as the league's best strong safety) in 1983, 1984, and 1985. **X**

start. After being crushed 32–0 by the New York Giants in the seventh game of the season, the Seahawks held a miserable 1–6 record. When Coach Patera met his players in the locker room after the game, he could manage only a short scolding. "Congratulations," he told them. "You're now the worst team in the National Football League. I'll see you tomorrow."

The next day, Patera put his players through a series of rigorous drills in full pads and was rewarded with a 19–3 victory the next week and wins in two of the following four games as well. But the Seahawks still finished in the AFC West cellar with a lowly 6–10 record. The next season began with two straight losses before a players' strike started in mid-September. By the time the NFL resumed play in late November, Patera had been fired. The disappointed Seahawks finished the shortened season 4–5 and were relieved to see it end.

STEVE LARGENT

WIDE RECEIVER
SEAHAWKS SEASONS: 1976-89
HEIGHT: 5-FOOT-11
WEIGHT: 187 POUNDS

Steve Largent was selected by the Houston Oilers in the fourth round of the 1976 NFL Draft, but after four disappointing preseason games, he was on the brink of being cut. Instead, he was traded to the brand-new Seattle Seahawks franchise, where he became one of the premier receivers in the game. Largent became quarterback Jim Zorn's go-to guy almost immediately. He was exceptionally sure-handed, totaling more than 1,000 yards in 8 of his 14 seasons with the Seahawks. He was the first Seahawks player selected to play in the Pro Bowl, which he did seven times, and the first retired player to be named to the team's Ring of Honor, which recognizes outstanding team players. When he retired in 1989, Largent held NFL records for career receptions (819), career receiving yards (13,089) and career touchdown receptions (100). He still holds franchise records for both single-season and career receiving yards. After his football days were over, Largent went on to serve four terms (or eight years) in the U.S. House of Representatives as a representative from his home state of Oklahoma

FORT KNOX

X ---------------------------------

X Halfback Curt Warner had a monster season as a rookie in 1983, carrying the ball more times (335) for more yards (1,449) and more touchdowns (13) than he ever would again.

The 1983 season started with two new faces in Seattle: coach Chuck Knox, who had previously led both the Los Angeles Rams and the Buffalo Bills to winning records, and running back Curt Warner, who had led Penn State University to the national college championship the year before and been selected by Seattle with the third overall pick in the 1983 NFL Draft. Warner was poised to play a prominent role in Knox's new offensive scheme.

Jim Zorn, however, would not. Injuries had hobbled the quarterback in 1982 and were hurting his performance in 1983 as well. When a pass intended for Warner fell to the ground three feet away from the running back just before halftime in Week 8, Zorn could tell by his coach's reaction that it was over. The second half of the game started with Dave Krieg under center. "I just had a sense that they were waiting for me to do something so they could put Dave in there," Zorn said later. "It was a lot more difficult being demoted than being cut."

Krieg threw two touchdowns in the second half of that game and earned the starting job for the rest of the season. With the help of Warner, who ran for an astonishing 1,449 yards, and kicker Norm Johnson, who tallied 103 points during the season, Krieg led the Seahawks to a 9–7 season record and their first trip to the playoffs.

Krieg delivered a near-perfect performance in the first round, completing 12 of 13 passes and tossing 3 touchdowns as the Seahawks crushed the Denver Broncos 31–7. But few people thought he could pull off the same magic against the Miami Dolphins the next week. And when Seattle fell behind by three points with less than four minutes remaining in the fourth quarter, it didn't look good. Then Krieg connected with Largent twice to set up a Warner touchdown run for a 24–20 lead. A Johnson field goal sealed the thrilling 27–20 victory, which Largent called "one of the best games the Seahawks ever played," and the team traveled to Los Angeles to face the Raiders in the AFC Championship Game. Although the Seahawks lost that contest 30–14, they had proven themselves to be a force.

The 1984 season started with hopes of making it to the Super Bowl. But as the Seahawks routed the Cleveland Browns 33–0 in the season opener, Warner went down with

X Dave Krieg (pictured) and the Seahawks fell to the Raiders in the 1983 playoffs but topped their rivals in a 1984 postseason rematch.

CHUCK KNOX

COACH
SEAHAWKS SEASONS: 1983-91

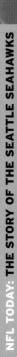

By the time Chuck Knox signed on as the head coach of the Seattle Seahawks in 1983, he had already been on NFL sidelines for more than 20 years and had served as head coach of the Los Angeles (now St. Louis) Rams and the Buffalo Bills for the previous 10. He inherited a veteran-heavy Seahawks team that had posted winning records only twice and had not yet played in a postseason game. When he came to Seattle, Knox laid down a whole new set of rules for the players—and immediately found success. In his first season with the Seahawks, the no-nonsense coach led Seattle to a 9–7 record and took the team within one game of the Super Bowl. Knox, who stayed in Seattle for nine seasons, returned to the playoffs three more times during his tenure with the team. He compiled an 80–63 record with the Seahawks and a 186–147–1 record as a professional coach. In 2005, Knox was inducted into the Seahawks' Ring of Honor, joining the company of eight of his former players.

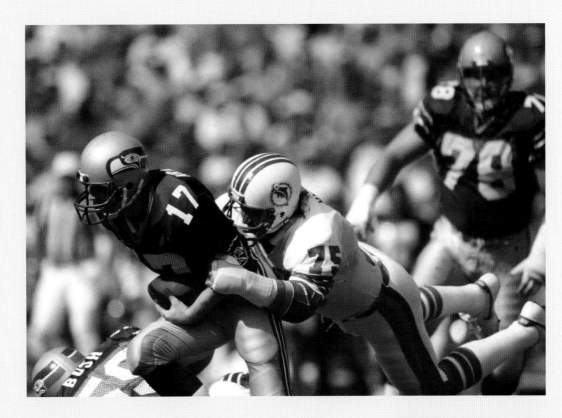

a season-ending injury, a torn ligament in his knee. "When it happened, the place went dead silent," safety Paul Moyer recalled. "Really quiet."

Losing Warner put more of the offensive burden on Krieg and a trio of backup running backs—David Hughes, Eric Lane, and Dan Doornink—but it didn't prevent the Seahawks from posting a 12–4 record and marching back to Los Angeles for a rematch with the Raiders in the opening round of the playoffs. This time, Seattle won and went on to face the Dolphins, who were in no mood for a repeat of the previous year. Miami crushed Seattle 31–10.

X The 1984 playoffs featured a clash between the two most distantly separated teams in the NFL, as the Seahawks traveled nearly 2,800 miles to Miami, only to get thumped by the Dolphins.

X Brian Blades made the Pro Bowl in his second NFL season (1989) and remained a Seahawks standout for more than a decade, topping 1,000 receiving yards in 4 different seasons.

Seattle didn't return to the playoffs until 1987. But as the Seahawks were building records of 8–8 in 1985 and 10–6 in 1986, they were also quietly beefing up their defense. Safety Eugene Robinson had joined Easley in the defensive secondary, and defensive end Jacob Green got some help from linebackers Tony Woods and Brian Bosworth, both products of the 1987 NFL Draft. With the impressive performance from the defense, and with Warner back in the lineup, Seattle returned to the playoffs with a 9–6 record, only to lose a heartbreaker in overtime to the Houston Oilers.

In 1988, speedy wide receiver Brian Blades and powerful tight end Mike Tice helped the aging Largent lead the offense. The Seahawks' 9–7 record was good enough to clinch their first AFC West championship title and another trip to the playoffs, but once again, Seattle couldn't get beyond the first round, this time losing to the Super Bowl-bound Cincinnati Bengals, 21–13.

That was the beginning of the end for Coach Knox and his Seahawks. Largent retired after the 1989 season. Warner left that same year to play one final season with the Los Angeles Rams. Two years later, Krieg left town too, and Coach Knox—who had compiled an 80–63 record and taken the Seahawks to the playoffs four times during his nine-year tenure—was

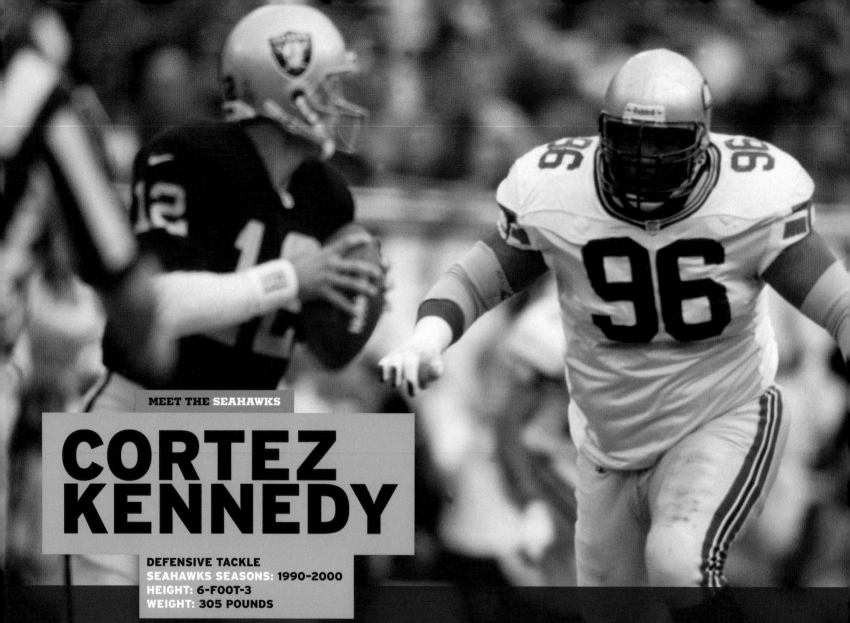

CORTEZ KENNEDY

DEFENSIVE TACKLE
SEAHAWKS SEASONS: 1990-2000
HEIGHT: 6-FOOT-3
WEIGHT: 305 POUNDS

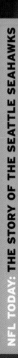

Cortez Kennedy almost missed his first season in Seattle. The All-American from the University of Miami had been selected by the Seahawks with the third overall pick in the 1990 NFL Draft—but then he didn't sign a contract with his new team until two days before the start of the regular season. That holdout resulted in a lackluster rookie campaign, with only 1 sack and 48 tackles, but it didn't hurt the rest of his career in Seattle. Kennedy, who played an entire decade with the Seahawks before retiring in 2000, "lived up to all our expectations," said coach Chuck Knox. The durable lineman played in 167 games, was named to 8 Pro Bowls, and was honored as an All-Pro 3 times. Many consider him to be one of the best defensive tackles ever to have played in the NFL, and many more believe that he should be voted into the Pro Football Hall of Fame. (In 2007, his first year of eligibility, he was among 26 semifinalists up for the honor.) Kennedy has already been inducted into the Seahawks' prestigious Ring of Honor.

fired after a 7–9 showing in 1991. Yet Knox remained thankful for his time with the Seahawks. "The fans here are the best fans of all the places I've been," he said. Knox left Seattle with the distinction of being the first head coach in NFL history to have won division titles with three different teams.

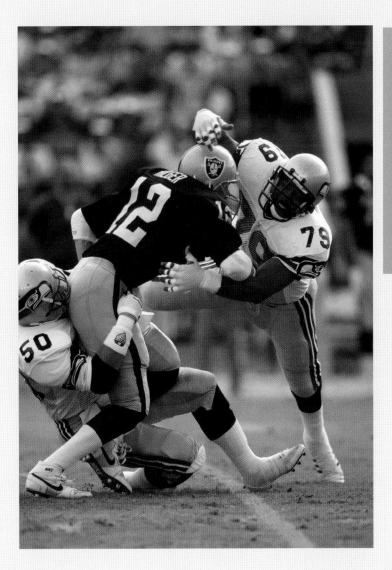

X Among the most feared pass rushers of the '80s, Jacob Green (number 79) officially notched 97.5 career quaterback sacks, even though the NFL did not count sacks until his third season (1982).

THE SEAHAWKS SLIDE

The only star left in Seattle when Tom Flores took over as head coach in 1992 was defensive tackle Cortez Kennedy, who led one of the best defenses in the league and was honored as the NFL's Defensive Player of the Year. But with a trio of inexperienced quarterbacks trying to lead the offense, Kennedy's efforts were wasted. The 140 total points that the Seahawks scored in that miserable 2–14 season set an NFL record for fewest points scored. "It was ugly," said Paul Moyer, a former Seahawks safety who had returned to Seattle to coach the secondary that season. "It was the most inept offense in the history of the NFL."

The silver lining to the Seahawks' dramatic slide was the opportunity to use the second pick of the 1993 NFL Draft to get Rick Mirer, a promising quarterback out of the University of Notre Dame. Mirer started every game for the 1993 Seahawks. After the dismal offensive performance the year before, Mirer's 2,833 passing yards (an NFL rookie record that broke the previous mark set by Jim Zorn in 1976)

ON THE SIDELINES

BACK TO THE PACK

Mike Holmgren was a beloved figure in Green Bay, Wisconsin. Green Bay Packers fans so adored the coach who had taken their team back to a Super Bowl victory in 1996 that they named a street near Lambeau Field after him. But after Holmgren moved to Seattle, he saw that the 1999 schedule included a game against the Packers in Green Bay, and he wasn't sure how it would feel to return. As it turned out, it felt great: Holmgren's Seahawks defeated the Packers in a 27–7 rout that included four Brett Favre interceptions and a warmer-than-expected reception from the fans. A friendly rivalry between the two teams developed over the years, especially when Favre's former backup Matt Hasselbeck was sent to Seattle in 2001, and one-time Seattle running back Ahman Green was traded to the Packers in 1999. The two teams have since met six more times, including a playoff game in 2004 in which Hasselbeck threw an interception to his former teammates in overtime, ending Seattle's season and sending the Packers to the next round of the playoffs.

and 12 touchdowns were cause for celebration in Seattle. With running back Chris Warren also breaking out with 1,072 rushing yards, Seattle improved to 6–10.

But that was the best that the Seahawks—and Mirer— could do. The flashy quarterback may have earned accolades for his stellar rookie year, but he didn't live up to the hype in subsequent seasons. Even after Dennis Erickson took over as head coach in 1995 and designed a new offensive system around Mirer and the speedy receiving trio of Blades, Ricky Proehl, and Joey Galloway, the Seahawks finished a mediocre 8–8. After a 1–4 start in 1996, Mirer was benched in favor of journeyman passer John Friesz.

Mirer was traded away in 1997 and replaced by 40-year-old veteran Warren Moon. Although Mirer had not lived up to expectations, his replacement exceeded them. Moon, who started the 1997 season as Friesz's backup, took over in the second week and proceeded to set new team records for completions (313) and passing yards (3,678). "I wish I knew what it was [that keeps Moon going]," Coach Erickson said, "because I'd bottle it up and sell it out of my office."

Moon started for two seasons in Seattle. He and fiery running back Ricky Watters, a free-agent signing prior to the 1998 season, brought the Seahawks to the brink of

X Veteran halfback Ricky Watters made NFL history in 1998 by becoming the first player ever to rush for more than 1,000 yards in a season for 3 different teams.

contention, but with an 8–8 finish in 1998, the team just missed the playoffs for the 10th straight season. Erickson was fired, Moon was released, and the Seahawks started the last season of the century with both a new coach and a new quarterback.

Seahawks owner Paul Allen had high hopes when he hired Mike Holmgren away from Green Bay, where Holmgren had led the Packers out of a nine-year slump and to a pair of Super Bowl appearances in 1996 and 1997. Holmgren elevated backup quarterback Jon Kitna to the starting position and brought in sure-handed wide receiver Sean Dawkins to help him out. The Seahawks went 9–7 in 1999 and finally broke back into the playoffs. But when Seattle hosted Miami in the AFC Wild Card game—the last game ever played in the Seahawks' Kingdome, which was demolished to make way for a new stadium—the Dolphins triumphed 20–17.

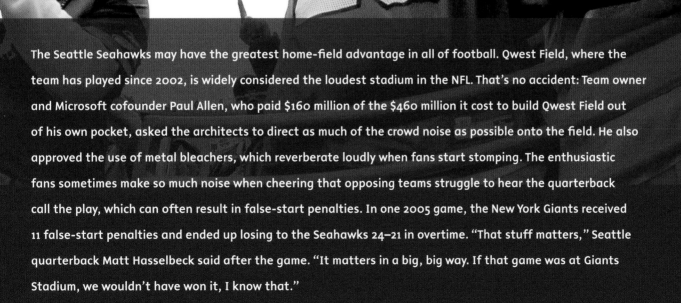

BRING ON THE NOISE

The Seattle Seahawks may have the greatest home-field advantage in all of football. Qwest Field, where the team has played since 2002, is widely considered the loudest stadium in the NFL. That's no accident: Team owner and Microsoft cofounder Paul Allen, who paid $160 million of the $460 million it cost to build Qwest Field out of his own pocket, asked the architects to direct as much of the crowd noise as possible onto the field. He also approved the use of metal bleachers, which reverberate loudly when fans start stomping. The enthusiastic fans sometimes make so much noise when cheering that opposing teams struggle to hear the quarterback call the play, which can often result in false-start penalties. In one 2005 game, the New York Giants received 11 false-start penalties and ended up losing to the Seahawks 24–21 in overtime. "That stuff matters," Seattle quarterback Matt Hasselbeck said after the game. "It matters in a big, big way. If that game was at Giants Stadium, we wouldn't have won it, I know that."

[31]

X   Although 6-foot-4 receiver Sean Dawkins showed flashes of brilliance during his two seasons in Seattle (1999 and 2000), he never became the superstar many fans had hoped for.

The hope of that season turned into frustration as the momentum Seattle had been building stalled during the next few years. Coach Holmgren brought in quarterback Trent Dilfer, who had won a Super Bowl with the Baltimore Ravens, to help, but when the 2002 campaign ended with a 7–9 record, the Seahawks watched the playoffs from home for the third straight season.

Never highly regarded as a passer, quarterback Trent Dilfer saw limited action in Seattle but made the most of his opportunities, going 8–4 there as a starter. X

SUPER BOWL
BOUND

Staying at home was not an option in 2003. That year, Matt Hasselbeck, who had played for Holmgren back in Green Bay, took over as Seattle's starting quarterback. With fleet-footed running back Shaun Alexander in the backfield and a pair of talented receivers—Koren Robinson and Darrell Jackson—waiting for him downfield, Hasselbeck led the team to a 10–6 record, including a franchise-first 8–0 record at home. One of the most memorable of those wins came on September 21 against the Seahawks' rivals, the St. Louis Rams. Alexander missed the first quarter of the game to be with his wife during the birth of their first daughter, but he sped to the stadium with a police escort in time to play in the second quarter and added 58 yards rushing in a narrow 24–23 victory.

Hasselbeck went head-to-head against Brett Favre, his former mentor in Green Bay, in the first round of the playoffs that year. On a frigid December day at Green Bay's Lambeau Field, the two teams battled back and forth to end regulation play at 20–20. When the Seahawks won the coin toss before overtime began, Hasselbeck confidently said, "We want the ball, and we're gonna score"—a statement that was picked up by the referee's microphone and broadcasted across the stadium and over the television networks. The young quarterback wished he could eat his words when, just

X Before making his famous overtime guarantee, Matt Hasselbeck gave a star-making performance in Seattle's 2003 playoff game against Green Bay, passing for more than 300 yards.

MATT HASSELBECK

QUARTERBACK
SEAHAWKS SEASONS: 2001–PRESENT
HEIGHT: 6-FOOT-4
WEIGHT: 223 POUNDS

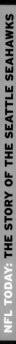

NFL TODAY: THE STORY OF THE SEATTLE SEAHAWKS

It was Matt Hasselbeck's misfortune to be drafted by the Green Bay Packers. For two seasons, he served as a backup to Brett Favre, who held the NFL record for most consecutive games started, and threw a grand total of only 29 passes. But then, in March 2001, Hasselbeck was traded to the Seattle Seahawks and given the opportunity to step into the starter's role. Hasselbeck was ready. He passed for more than 2,000 yards and 7 touchdowns in 2001. Those numbers increased each season, as he threw 24 touchdowns in Seattle's Super Bowl season in 2005 and had a career-high 28 in 2007. Hasselbeck, whose father was a tight end for the New England Patriots in the 1970s and '80s, was injured twice in the 2006 season—first when a linebacker rolled over his right leg, then when he broke several fingers on his left (non-throwing) hand. Still, the gutsy quarterback led the Seahawks to the playoffs in both 2006 and 2007 and by 2008 was being described by offensive coordinator Gil Haskell as "the best player on our team."

a few plays later, he launched a pass that was intercepted by Packers cornerback Al Harris, who ran it back for a touchdown and a 33–27 Green Bay victory.

With the offense firing on all cylinders, the Seahawks bulked up defensively in the off-season, drafting tackle Marcus Tubbs to help cornerback Marcus Trufant and linebackers Chad Brown and Orlando Huff. Collectively, the defense intercepted 23 passes, sacked opposing quarterbacks 36 times, and recovered 20 fumbles in 2004. With Hasselbeck passing for 3,382 yards and Alexander rushing for 1,696 more, the Seahawks returned to the playoffs.

X Linebacker Orlando Huff contributed to the Seahawks' offense in 2003 by scoring both a safety and a fumble-recovery touchdown.

X Chad Brown was known for both his punishing tackles and his love of snakes—away from football, the linebacker bred and sold the reptiles as a hobby.

Seattle's Wild Card game against the St. Louis Rams once again came down to the wire. The Rams led 27–20 with less than a minute left to play, but Hasselbeck drove the Seahawks down to the five-yard line. On fourth down, with 4 yards to go and 27 seconds on the clock, Hasselbeck put up a pass that thudded to the ground. Seattle's season ended short of the Super Bowl once more.

When the Seahawks started the 2005 season 2–2, many fans predicted that the year would end in disappointment

STREAKING TO THE SUPER BOWL

Losing the first game of the 2005 season was not the ideal start for a team that had hopes of making it to the Super Bowl for the first time. By Week 4, the Seahawks owned a mediocre 2–2 record. But after the following week's 37–31 victory over its division rivals, the St. Louis Rams, Seattle just couldn't lose. The team trounced the Houston Texans 42–10 in Week 6 and beat the Dallas Cowboys 13–10 with a last-minute field goal in Week 7. After a week off, they topped the Arizona Cardinals 33–19, then earned another win against the Rams with a mark of 31–16. The winning streak continued for 11 weeks, lasting through the next-to-last game of the season. The Seahawks' unstoppable offense, led by quarterback Matt Hasselbeck and running back Shaun Alexander, put 40 or more points on the board 3 times, including a 42–0 shutout against the Philadelphia Eagles. Seattle lost its final game, 23–17, in Green Bay, but had already clinched a playoff berth. That was all the team needed to reach Super Bowl XL.

SHAUN ALEXANDER

RUNNING BACK
SEAHAWKS SEASONS: 2000-07
HEIGHT: 5-FOOT-11
WEIGHT: 225 POUNDS

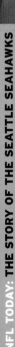

The 2005 season was a big one for Shaun Alexander. He broke records all season long, including the NFL mark for touchdowns scored in a season (28), and he ran away with the league rushing title with 1,880 yards. He also led the league in touchdowns, points scored, and Pro Bowl votes, and he beat out Indianapolis Colts star quarterback Peyton Manning for the NFL MVP award. But there were yet more honors in store for Alexander, who was selected by the Seahawks with the 19th pick of the 2000 NFL Draft after an award-winning college career at the University of Alabama. In December 2005, he made the cover of *Sports Illustrated*, becoming the first Seahawks player ever to earn the coveted spot on the weekly sports magazine. Unfortunately, after being rewarded with a stunning 8-year, $62-million contract, Alexander broke a bone in his foot in the third game of the 2006 season, limiting him to fewer than 900 yards in 10 games. After gaining only 716 yards and scoring just 5 total touchdowns in 2007, Alexander was released by the team.

again. But after losing to the Washington Redskins in overtime on October 2, Seattle put together an incredible string of 11 straight wins, including a 42–0 shredding of the Philadelphia Eagles. "This year, the ball is bouncing a little bit for us," Coach Holmgren said during the winning streak. "We're getting wins that in years past might have slipped away."

By season's end, the Seahawks had compiled a 13–3 record, which put them atop the NFC West Division (which the Seahawks had joined in 2002). Another first-round elimination wasn't an option for these determined Seahawks; two decades after its last playoff victory, Seattle defeated both the Redskins and the Carolina Panthers to reach Super Bowl XL, where it faced a red-hot Pittsburgh Steelers team. The game was close until the Steelers scored a touchdown in the fourth quarter that put Pittsburgh up 21–10. The Seahawks could not close the gap and returned to Seattle without the coveted Lombardi Trophy.

The loss was disappointing, but Seattle was determined to show its resilience. With Hasselbeck and Alexander complemented by receiver Deion Branch and fullback Mack Strong, the Seahawks returned to the playoffs again in 2006. Although the Chicago Bears beat them in a second-round matchup, the Seahawks soared to another NFC West title for

X Thanks to such players as receiver Deion Branch (number 83), the Seahawks appeared in the playoffs every season from 2002 to 2007.

the fourth consecutive season in 2007. But when it came time for the playoffs, the Seahawks saw their season end short of the Super Bowl once again with a 42–20 playoff drubbing at the hands of Green Bay.

That playoff loss seemed to throw the Seahawks off track. Hasselbeck struggled with injuries in 2008, and the team started 2–9 before finishing far from postseason contention in Coach Holmgren's final season in Seattle. By the end of the painful year, players such as Hasselbeck, Trufant, and linebacker Lofa Tatupu could only rededicate themselves to a turnaround in 2009.

THE 12TH MAN

Twelve season-ticket holders from the Seahawks' inaugural season in 1976 gathered in the end zone of Seattle's Qwest Field on October 12, 2003. Together, they hoisted a blue flag emblazoned with the number 12 up a towering new flagpole. At every home game since then, that same flag in the southern end zone has been raised by a former Seahawks player or other local celebrity as part of a pregame ritual that honors the Seahawks' fans, who are so important that the team has often referred to them as the "12th man." Seattle has a history of thanking its faithful followers. In 1984, it became the first professional sports team to retire a jersey number in honor of its fans when it hung a number 12 jersey from the rafters of the Kingdome. And in 2005, after fan noise flustered the New York Giants in a critical game, contributing to a Seahawks win and a trip to the Super Bowl, head coach Mike Holmgren presented an honorary game ball to the crowd in appreciation of its support.

ON THE SIDELINES

FOR THE BIRDS

The first thing fans at Seattle's Qwest Field see coming out of the tunnel at game time is Taima, an Augur hawk that has become a live mascot for the team. Taima, which means "thunder," leads the Seahawks out of the tunnel before every home game. Then the bird, which weighs about three pounds and has a four-and-a-half-foot wingspan, swoops across the field at speeds of between 80 and 100 miles per hour before meeting up with its trainer, David Knutson, on the sidelines. Taima, who was hatched on April 21, 2005, at the World Bird Sanctuary in St. Louis, Missouri, started flying through the 67,000-seat stadium at the start of the 2005 season when the bird was just 5 months old. Fans and players quickly developed a bond with the graceful hawk. Knutson spent as much time as he could during the games roaming the sidelines with Taima on his hand, stopping to let spectators stroke the bird and say hello. "It's almost become like a buddha, where people rub his belly for good luck," Knutson said. "The fans love that bird."

For more than 30 years, the Seattle Seahawks have taken

fans in the Pacific Northwest for an exciting ride. Despite

the frustrations experienced along the way, the team has

always given its fans hope for the future. With a string of

successful seasons in the works, today's Seahawks hope to

soon enhance the natural beauty of their hometown with the

shine of a Super Bowl trophy.

X Although smaller than the average linebacker, Lofa Tatupu's sure tackling, good hands, and nonstop hustle made him a Seahawks star.

INDEX